Profiles of the Presidents

RICHARD
M. NIXON

★ ★ ★

Profiles of the Presidents

RICHARD
M. NIXON

by Robert Green

Content Adviser: Marlene Smith-Baranzini, Former Editor, *California History Quarterly*
Reading Adviser: Dr. Linda D. Labbo, Department of Reading Education, College of Education, The University of Georgia

Compass Point Books
3109 West 50th Street, #115
Minneapolis, MN 55410

Visit Compass Point Books on the Internet at *www.compasspointbooks.com*
or e-mail your request to *custserv@compasspointbooks.com*

Photographs ©: Hulton/Archive by Getty Images, cover, 1, 8, 19, 29, 31, 41, 44, 57 (top right), 58 (left and bottom right); National Archives and Records Administration, 6, 14; Photo Courtesy of the Richard Nixon Library, 7, 10, 24, 35 (top), 39; Wally McNamee/Corbis, 9, 35 (bottom), 49, 59 (left); Bettmann/Corbis, 11, 13 (all), 15, 16 (all), 17, 18, 20, 21, 22, 23, 26, 27, 28, 33, 36, 38, 40, 45, 55 (left), 56 (left), 57 (left); Mark E. Gibson/Corbis, 12, 54; Corbis, 25, 34, 42; LBJ Library Photo by Yoichi R. Okamoto, 30; Topham Picturepoint, 32, 46, 47; Leif Skoogfors/Corbis, 37; Courtesy Gerald R. Ford Library and Museum, 48; Richard Cummins/Corbis, 50; Courtesy Franklin D. Roosevelt Library, 55 (right); Galen Rowell/Corbis, 56 (right); NASA, 57 (bottom right), 59 (right); Courtesy Intel Museum Archives and Collections, 58 (top right); Reuters NewMedia Inc./Corbis, 59 (bottom right).

Editors: E. Russell Primm, Emily J. Dolbear, Melissa McDaniel, and Catherine Neitge
Photo Researchers: Image Select International and Svetlana Zhurkina
Photo Selector: Linda S. Koutris
Designer/Page Production: The Design Lab/Les Tranby
Cartographer: XNR Productions, Inc.

Library of Congress Cataloging-in-Publication Data
Green, Robert.
   Richard M. Nixon / by Robert Green.
      v. cm.— (Profiles of the presidents)
Includes bibliographical references (p.) and index.
Contents: California Quaker—On the trail of the red menace—So close to the top—Political wilderness—The Nixon years—Making peace with the communists—Watergate—Glossary—Did you know?—Richard M. Nixon's life at a glance—Richard M. Nixon's life and times— World events—Understanding Richard M. Nixon and his presidency.
   ISBN 0-7565-0281-0
   1. Nixon, Richard M. (Richard Milhous), 1913–1994—Juvenile literature. 2. Presidents—United States—Biography—Juvenile literature. [1. Nixon, Richard M. (Richard Milhous), 1913–1994 2. Presidents.]
I. Title. II. Series.
   E856 .G74 2003
   973.924'092—dc21   2002010045

Table of Contents

★ ★ ★

NOTE: In this book, words that are defined in the glossary are in **bold** *the first time they appear in the text.*

"I Am Not a Crook"

★ ★ ★

When Richard Nixon was elected president in 1968, America seemed to be at war with itself. Students protested American involvement in the Vietnam War in Southeast Asia. Riots broke out in cities because of tensions between

A student ▸ protester offering a flower to a military policeman during a demonstration against the Vietnam War

◄ *Voters saw Nixon as the leader who would unite America and end the Vietnam War.*

white and black Americans. Crime rates soared, and fewer Americans felt safe.

Voters turned to Richard Nixon to solve these troubles. Nixon, a Republican, pledged to end the war in Vietnam and to bring American soldiers home. He also promised "to bring us together." He said he would combat the growing distrust that many Americans had for the government.

As president, Nixon succeeded in ending U.S. involvement in Vietnam. He also managed to ease American tensions with the powerful nations of China and the Soviet Union.

By and large, Americans liked Nixon. When he ran for reelection in 1972, he won with ease.

Then, slowly, everything crumbled. News of political spying and dirty tricks began to leak to the press. Criminal activity including burglary was traced back to the White House.

Soon, it became clear that Nixon knew about the illegal activities of his aides. Nixon resigned, or left office. He is the only U.S. president ever to have resigned. "I am not a crook," he proclaimed. Americans, however, expected more than that from their president.

Richard Nixon is the only president to have resigned. ▶

Nixon giving a
farewell speech to
his staff the day
after resigning

Nixon had entered the White House pledging to
bring the country together. Instead, he dragged the
United States into one of the biggest political scandals in
its history. His name would forever be linked with what
became known as Watergate.

California Quaker

★ ★ ★

Richard Milhous Nixon was born in the small town of Yorba Linda, California, on January 9, 1913. He grew up in the nearby town of Whittier, where his father ran a gas station and a store. Richard's parents, Francis and Hannah, had two other sons. Sadly, both of Richard's brothers died during childhood.

Francis and Hannah Nixon on their wedding day ▾

The Nixons belonged to the Quaker religion. They often went to the local Friends Meeting House, which is the church that Quakers attend. A meetinghouse has no priest or minister. Instead, every person has the chance to speak. Richard Nixon proved to be an able speaker.

After graduating from high school, Nixon attended Whittier College, a local Quaker college. He majored in history at Whittier and was elected student body president. Nixon was something of a straight arrow, an honest type of guy who was willing to work very hard for success.

▾ *Nixon (back row, center) with fellow football players at Whittier College*

Nixon was awarded a scholarship to Duke University in 1934.

His hard work in school paid off. Nixon won a scholarship to study law at Duke University in North Carolina after graduating from Whittier in 1934. Like so many other kids without a lot of money, Nixon relied on his intelligence and hard work to get ahead.

At Duke, he worked part time to earn money. His confidence grew as he discovered that he could hold his own in the law school. He was elected president of the Duke Bar Association, a club for law students. He graduated third in his class.

After finishing law school, Nixon moved back to Whittier and joined the town's oldest law firm. He soon became a successful lawyer.

◀ *Nixon returned to his home in Whittier after graduating from law school.*

Nixon considered himself a private man, someone who was shy and did not like attention. If that was true, he hid it well. While working as a lawyer in Whittier, Nixon started acting in plays. He was already a good speaker, and he also proved to be a gifted actor. He could also make people laugh.

In the local theater, he met a teacher named Thelma Catherine Ryan. She preferred the name Pat. Pat Ryan had a naturalness about her that comforted Nixon. In 1940, Richard and Pat were married.

◀ *Richard Nixon and Pat Ryan hold their marriage license shortly before their 1940 wedding.*

The Rising Star

★   ★   ★

In 1941, the United States entered World War II (1939–1945). The conflict affected almost every American. Nixon took a job in Washington, D.C., working for a government agency that rationed tires. During the war, the government made sure the army got all the food and supplies it needed by rationing, or limiting, how much people at home got.

Nixon worked for a ▶
government agency
that rationed tires
during World War II.

Nixon found the way the agency worked kind of baffling. He wondered why so much paperwork was needed to ration tires.

Nixon next joined the U.S. Navy and was soon sent to the South Pacific. There Nixon worked for Naval Air Transport, which ferried soldiers and supplies to the front lines. This job gave him some experi-

▲ *Nixon as a lieutenant commander in the navy*

ence in organizing men and materials. By the time Nixon left the navy in 1946, he had risen to the rank of lieutenant commander.

During World War II, the United States had fought on the same side as the **Soviet Union**. Even before the war ended in 1945, however, tensions were increasing between the two nations. The Soviet Union had been formed in 1922, when Russia and other countries in

Eastern Europe and central Asia combined. The Soviet Union was a **communist** country. Many Americans did not like communists or trust countries with communist governments. They feared that other countries around the world would also become communist.

Joseph Stalin, Communist leader of the Soviet Union

In California, the Republicans were looking for a candidate to run against the Democratic congressman Jerry Voorhis. They approached Nixon, and he threw himself into the race. During the campaign, Nixon attacked Voorhis's patriotism. He hinted that Voorhis was linked to communists in the

Congressman Richard Nixon in 1949

United States. Nixon easily won the election.

Representative Richard Nixon was well suited to the times. In the 1940s, many Americans were afraid of communism. People thought there were communists everywhere. Nixon became a national figure by searching for communist spies.

Members of Congress serve on **committees**, which tackle different problems. Nixon landed some important committee jobs. For one committee, he was sent to Europe to study how American money could help rebuild European countries that had been shattered by World War II.

This idea was known as the Marshall Plan, named for Secretary of State George C. Marshall. The plan also had a political edge. Many government officials were afraid that Europeans, facing big war debts and destroyed cities, might turn to communism. U.S. officials hoped that by helping Europeans rebuild,

▼ These stars and stripes were stamped on each package of food or supplies sent to European nations devastated by World War II.

FOR EUROPEAN RECOVERY

SUPPLIED BY THE

UNITED STATES OF AMERICA

Nixon (far right) with
other members of the
House Un-American
Activities Committee

they would keep communism out of Western Europe.

Nixon learned much during his visits to Europe. They helped spark his lifelong interest in **foreign affairs.**

Nixon was also appointed to the House Un-American Activities Committee. This committee had been set up to look into communist activities in the United States. Nixon became a leading member of the committee.

The committee held hearings to determine just who was a communist and who was not. They feared there might be communists in the government who could reveal American secrets to the Soviet Union.

When a former State Department official named Alger Hiss was found to be an active Communist Party member, Nixon had found his mark. He hammered away at Hiss. Nixon questioned witnesses and collected evidence against Hiss. Alger Hiss was later convicted of lying to the committee.

Some people thought the House Un-American Activities Committee was reckless. They said it ruined lives by accusing people of being communists without any proof. They also pointed out that Americans have the right to express their political beliefs, even if they are communists. Many people ignored these complaints. At the time, hounding suspected communists was very popular among Americans.

▼ *Alger Hiss*

So Close to the Top

★   ★   ★

Nixon was a popular congressman, and the Alger Hiss case had brought him national attention. Nixon decided to run for the U.S. Senate in 1950. The Democratic **candidate** was Congresswoman Helen Gahagan Douglas.

Helen Gahagan Douglas, whom Nixon renamed "the pink lady"

Nixon nicknamed Douglas "the pink lady." Because communists were often called "reds," calling someone "pink" implied that they were somehow in favor of communism.

Nixon won the election. The way he won his elections, however, was starting to bother some people. They thought he was too quick to label people communists.

Still, Nixon was a rising star in the Republican Party. He had been a senator for just two years when presidential candidate General Dwight D. Eisenhower asked him to be his running mate. Nixon jumped at the chance. He was just thirty-nine years old.

During the presidential campaign, questions arose about Nixon's ethics. It was revealed that some people had given Nixon money to pay his expenses while he was a senator. Americans wondered whether Nixon had done these people political favors in exchange for the money.

▲ *Richard and Pat Nixon with daughter Julie, as the Nixons cast votes in the 1950 election*

To defend himself, Nixon gave a speech on television. He explained that he did not have a rich lifestyle. He said that his wife did not have a mink coat, "but she does have a respectable Republican cloth coat." Viewers liked what he said. Above all, they liked the part where Nixon talked about his dog, Checkers. His speech was a huge success. Officials also decided that he had not broken any laws in taking the money.

Nixon giving his televised "Checkers" speech

◄ *President Eisenhower (left) and Vice President Richard Nixon*

Eisenhower and Nixon were elected in 1952. Eisenhower was the nation's greatest hero from World War II. He also had a nice grandfatherly image. What he lacked was political experience.

Because of Eisenhower's lack of experience, many of the political decisions fell to Nixon. He performed these duties with relish. Nixon became a loud voice for Republican causes. He also lined up support for the president.

Nixon's aggressive ways also had a downside. Many Democrats—and some Republicans—who had voted for Eisenhower didn't like Nixon. Some Republicans believed that Eisenhower should choose a different running mate when he ran for reelection in 1956. Nixon also had many supporters, though. Eisenhower stuck with him, and the two were reelected.

Nixon's two terms as vice president were a great experience for him. Vice presidents are often frustrated because they have little real power. Eisenhower, however, trusted Nixon's judgment. The president was also sick quite often. As a result, Nixon had real power and responsibilities.

During Nixon's eight years as vice president, he visited fifty-six countries. These experiences deepened his understanding of foreign affairs.

On his travels, Nixon was open about his dislike of communism. In the South American country of Venezuela, protesters pelted Nixon and his wife with stones as they drove through the streets. Eisenhower sent U.S. troops to protect the vice president. Americans admired the way Nixon handled himself, taking the violence in stride and not showing any fear.

Nixon spoke with ▶ Cuban leader Fidel Castro (left) during one of his many world trips as vice president.

◄ *Khrushchev (left) and Nixon during the "kitchen debate" in Moscow*

On a visit to Moscow, the capital of the Soviet Union, Nixon got into a **debate** with the Soviet leader, Nikita Khrushchev. The discussion took place at the American National Exhibition. Nixon stood in the kitchen of a model American home and fended off Khrushchev's hostile questions. The event became known as the "kitchen debate." It made Nixon even more popular at home.

As Eisenhower neared the end of his second term, Richard Nixon launched his own campaign to become the next president. He was the clear favorite among Republicans. Also, many people thought that the Democratic candidate, John F. Kennedy, was too young at forty-three to be elected president.

Newspaper reporters, however, were fascinated by Kennedy's youth and charm. Kennedy was witty and confident. Despite his youth, he had already served in both the House of Representatives and the Senate. When Kennedy and Nixon held a series of televised debates, Kennedy looked more relaxed. During one of the debates, Nixon, who was just getting over an illness, looked tired. Nixon had always been a good speaker. It had gotten him where he was. After watching the debates, many people decided to support Kennedy.

1960 presidential ▼ candidate John F. Kennedy

Nixon lost the election, and Kennedy became the youngest person ever to win the presidency. It was one of the closest presidential elections in American history. Nixon fumed about it. He believed that the press had unfairly favored Kennedy. Forever after, Richard Nixon would distrust

reporters. He always saw them as enemies who were trying to bring him down.

After the election, Nixon returned to California,
where he joined a large law firm in Los Angeles. He was
earning more at that time than in the previous fourteen
years of politics, and he even wrote a book about his
political experiences. Although Nixon made a good living
as a lawyer, he missed politics.

◀ *Richard Nixon*
congratulated
President-elect
Kennedy in
Florida, where
both men were
vacationing after
the election.

Edmund G. ▸
"Pat" Brown

In 1962, Nixon ran for governor of California. He ran against the popular Democratic governor, Edmund G. "Pat" Brown. Again, Nixon lost. Nixon was still bitter. He had been the favorite among Republicans for so many years. As vice president, he had been just one step away from the presidency of the United States.

After losing two elections, Nixon could see no future for himself in politics. He lashed out at the press. "You won't have Nixon to kick around anymore," he said, "because, gentlemen, this is my last press conference."

Nixon moved to New York City and took a job at a Wall Street law firm. He intended to make a very good living as a lawyer.

◄ *Nixon moved to New York City when he decided to quit politics.*

The pull of politics was just too strong, however. Nixon became active in the Republican Party of New York. He hosted fund-raising dinners and made speeches for candidates. Nixon worked hard for the party, and he helped get many Republicans elected. Once again, Nixon's name was on the lips of many Republicans.

As the 1968 presidential election neared, Nixon decided to make another run for the highest office in the land. President Lyndon Johnson, who succeeded Kennedy after his assassination, was facing constant criticism over the Vietnam War (1964–1975). He was tired of it and decided not to run for reelection.

Lyndon Johnson decided not to run for reelection in 1968.

This decision meant that Nixon would not have to run against a sitting president.

Nixon became the Republican candidate for president. The two other candidates in the election were Democratic senator Hubert Humphrey of Minnesota and Governor George Wallace of Alabama, who was running as an independent. Nixon tried to convince voters that his political views fell between those of Humphrey and Wallace. That way he might get the votes of Democrats who thought that Humphrey wouldn't do enough about the increasing crime rates. He might also get the votes of Republicans who thought Wallace was too extreme.

Nixon chose Maryland governor Spiro T. Agnew as his vice presidential running mate. They promised to find a way to bring Americans back together. Nixon said that he would take American troops out of Vietnam and that he would clamp down on crime. The combination was a winning one. After nearly a decade out of office, in 1968 Richard Nixon was elected the thirty-seventh president of the United States.

◄ *Pat Nixon looks on as her husband is sworn in as president on January 20, 1969.*

The Nixon Years

★ ★ ★

As president, Nixon had to deal with an unpopular war abroad and growing problems at home. Americans were becoming less trustful of their leaders. Many young people spoke out against the war in Vietnam. They were growing apart from older people.

The differences were plain for all to see. Young people grew their hair long and rejected their parents' val-

American soldiers ▶ were still in Vietnam when Nixon took office.

◄ The government's efforts to grant black citizens equal rights often sparked hostility among whites.

ues. Many African-Americans refused to accept the slow pace at which they were becoming full and equal citizens. Some turned to violence. Some whites also turned to violence to keep black Americans down. At times, Nixon faced these challenges well, but it was often a bumpy road.

Nixon believed that the government could be useful in solving social problems. He supported plans that gave African-Americans assistance in finding jobs and getting into colleges. Nixon also supported welfare, which helps the poor and other needy people.

These programs were not popular with all Republicans, especially in the South. Many **conservative** Republicans didn't think government should be involved in helping people directly. To help keep the support of these Republicans, Nixon tried to name two conservative Southerners to the U.S. Supreme Court. The U.S. Senate has to approve the president's choices. Both men were rejected because senators thought they would not uphold the rights of African-Americans.

By the time Nixon left the presidency, four men he had chosen were sitting on the Supreme Court. Nixon hoped that these justices would swing the Court in a conservative direction.

Nixon wanted to ▼ establish a Supreme Court with highly conservative judges.

Nixon was a strong supporter of women's rights. He appointed women to important jobs. The most important woman in shaping the president's image was his wife. Pat Nixon's popularity helped her husband's presidency. Nixon was often bitter toward members of the press, but Pat could charm them.

Nixon experienced some happy times during his presidency. In 1971, his daughter Patricia married a law student named Edward Finch Cox in an elegant wedding at the White House. In 1968, his other daughter, Julie, had married David Eisenhower, a grandson of Nixon's old boss, Dwight Eisenhower.

◀ Pat Nixon receiving an award from an African leader (above) and Richard Nixon with his daughter Patricia on her wedding day

Making Peace

★ ★ ★

The Vietnam War dominated Nixon's presidency from the start. Communist North Vietnam had been fighting noncommunist South Vietnam since 1959. The United States began sending troops in 1965 to help South Vietnam fight the war. By 1969, when Nixon took office, 550,000 American soldiers were serving in Vietnam.

Every night, the television news showed American soldiers fighting in Vietnamese villages and jungles. The

When Americans saw images such as this one, it made them frustrated that U.S. soldiers were risking their lives in South Vietnam.

names of soldiers killed in action were published every day in the newspapers. The war seemed to drag on endlessly. Many people couldn't understand why Americans should die to help South Vietnam.

The war divided Americans like no issue had since the Civil War nearly tore the nation apart in the 1860s. Many people were unkind to soldiers who had returned from Vietnam. Even some of those soldiers spoke out against the war.

◄ *A Vietnam veteran at an antiwar rally in 1970*

Colleges were often the center of antiwar protests. In 1970, Ohio National Guardsmen opened fire on protesters at Kent State University. Four students were killed. It was a nightmare for the president. Nixon was determined to get the United States out of Vietnam.

The first thing he wanted to do was ensure that fewer Americans were killed. To do this, he increased training for South Vietnamese soldiers. That way fewer Americans would be needed to fight the war in Vietnam, so fewer would die there.

The scene at Kent ▶ State University where National Guardsmen fired on protesters

Nixon and his national security adviser, Henry Kissinger, wanted to talk to the North Vietnamese about ending the war. Nixon, however, believed that North Vietnam would not agree to peace talks until their military was so weak that they knew they couldn't win the war.

To disrupt North Vietnamese supply lines, Nixon ordered secret bombings of the neighboring countries of Laos and Cambodia. He also approved military raids into these countries. When the public heard about these actions, the protests only became louder. It seemed that rather than ending the war, he was expanding it.

◄ *Nixon greeting National Security Adviser Henry Kissinger (left)*

Despite the uproar, Nixon achieved what he set out to do. By 1972, he had reduced the number of American troops in Vietnam to about thirty thousand. Peace talks had started.

During his time as president, Nixon

Laotian refugees ▲
fleeing their
homeland to
escape the
bombings

also tried to improve relations between the United States and the world's two major communist powers, China and the Soviet Union. Nixon sent Henry Kissinger to China to talk about a possible presidential visit.

Communists had taken over the Chinese government in 1949. The country's former noncommunist leaders fled to the small island of Taiwan, off the Chinese mainland. Since then, the United States had refused to accept the communist government in mainland China as the country's official government. The United States clung to the claim that the government in Taiwan was the only Chinese government.

Then, in 1972, Nixon announced that he would visit mainland China. This bold move caught people by surprise. Many were happy to hear the news. Nixon had made his career battling communists, but now he sensed the time was right to ease tensions.

Accompanied by Pat, Nixon arrived in February and met with communist leader Mao Tse-tung and other Chinese officials. After Nixon's trip, the United States established more normal relations with mainland China. This change was a relief to many Americans. China was backing North Vietnam in the Vietnam War. It had

◄ *Communist leader Mao Tse-tung and Nixon during the 1972 visit*

Nixon met with Soviet leader Leonid Brezhnev to discuss reducing weapons in both the United States and the Soviet Union.

always been possible that China might get involved in the war. Now it seemed less likely.

Following his success in China, Nixon turned his attention to the Soviet Union. For years, the United States and the Soviet Union had been building more and more **nuclear weapons** to use against each other. To try to slow down this dangerous buildup, Nixon and Soviet

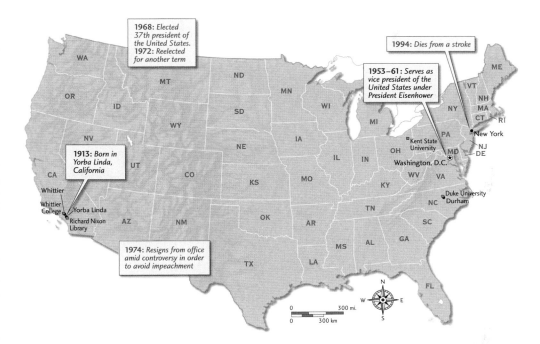

1968: *Elected 37th president of the United States.*
1972: *Reelected for another term*

1994: *Dies from a stroke*

1953–61: *Serves as vice president of the United States under President Eisenhower*

1913: *Born in Yorba Linda, California*

1974: *Resigns from office amid controversy in order to avoid impeachment*

leaders held talks. They agreed to limit the number of weapons their countries built.

Many Americans liked how Nixon had improved relations with China and the Soviet Union. As the presidential election of 1972 neared, the United States was very close to signing an agreement to bring the last troops home from Vietnam. Nixon was more popular than ever.

The Watergate Scandal

★ ★ ★

President Nixon had little time to campaign for reelection. His campaign was handled by the Committee to Reelect the President. His Democratic challenger, George McGovern, had trouble drumming up support even among Democrats. In the election, Nixon won every state except Massachusetts and the District of Columbia. He

Senator George ▼ McGovern (left), the Democratic candidate for president, and his running mate, Sargent Shriver

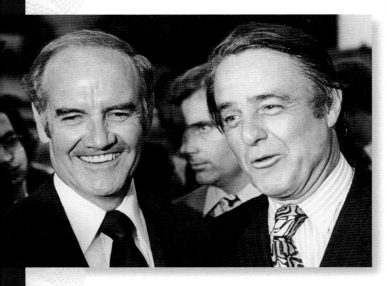

was easily elected to a second term as president.

Slowly, however, disturbing news about the Nixon White House leaked out. On June 17, 1972, several months before the election, burglars had broken into the Democratic National

Committee offices at the Watergate Hotel in Washington, D.C. The burglars were traced back to the White House. It seemed like Nixon's aides were trying to spy on the Democrats. Nixon said he didn't know anything about the Watergate break-in. He continued business as usual.

Law enforcement agents and reporters kept investigating the Watergate break-in, however. The story grew larger and larger. By 1973, the break-in and other wrongdoings had been traced as far up as Nixon's chief of staff. Nixon "cleaned house," and three of his most important aides left their jobs.

◄ *Nixon's top aides, including Chief of Staff H.R. Haldeman, were questioned about Watergate.*

During the same year, Nixon's vice president, Spiro Agnew, resigned after he was accused of tax evasion. It was painful for Americans to learn about the crimes of the men they had just reelected.

Later that year, a White House aide revealed that Nixon often secretly taped conversations in his office. The Senate committee that was investigating the Watergate scandal wanted to hear the audio tapes. Nixon refused to hand them over. He claimed they were private property. By that time, Nixon was standing almost entirely alone. He didn't even trust his closest advisers.

Nixon initially ▶ refused to hand over the tapes.

A man named Archibald Cox was in charge of the government's investigation of the Watergate scandal. When he said he would force Nixon to give up the tapes, the president ordered his **attorney general** to fire Cox. Instead, the attorney general quit. The public turned against Nixon. His desperate actions looked like those of a guilty man.

Finally, in 1974, the Supreme Court ruled that Nixon had to release the tapes. Meanwhile, Congress was preparing to **impeach** the president. This meant that they were charging him with serious crimes while in office. Nixon's

▼ *Nixon saying goodbye to the nation in his 1974 farewell speech*

attempts to escape the investigators had failed. He knew he could be forced from office. To avoid being charged, President Richard Nixon resigned on August 9, 1974.

Vice President Gerald Ford, who had replaced Spiro Agnew, was sworn in as president. Hoping to end the scandal, Ford granted Nixon a full **pardon.** This action meant that Nixon could not be tried on any criminal charges after leaving office. Many Americans were outraged by Ford's pardon.

Gerald Ford (below) ◄
*became president
and granted Nixon
a full pardon for
his involvement
in Watergate.*

News of Nixon's misdeeds only increased after he left office. It was revealed that he had created a list of his political enemies. He had ordered that the Federal Bureau of Investigation (FBI) and the Internal Revenue Service (IRS) harass his

enemies. He had also illegally listened in on the phone calls of reporters, his political enemies, and even White House staff members.

After he resigned, Nixon went home to California. Many people forgot that he had pulled American soldiers out of Vietnam and smoothed relations with China. They saw only a fearful, bitter man who had used illegal methods and dirty tricks to silence his critics.

▲ *Nixon in 1978, his first public appearance since resigning four years earlier*

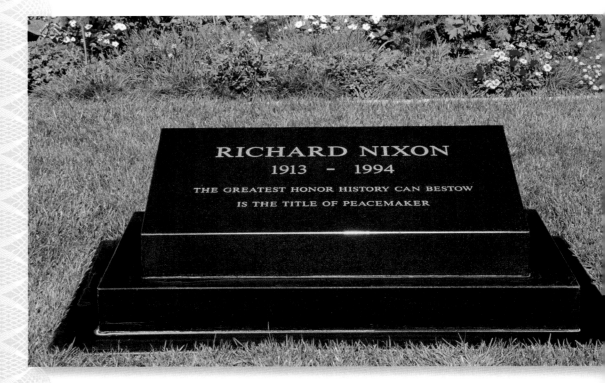

RICHARD NIXON
1913 — 1994
THE GREATEST HONOR HISTORY CAN BESTOW
IS THE TITLE OF PEACEMAKER

*Richard Milhous ▲
Nixon's grave in
Yorba Linda,
California*

In the years after Nixon left office, he wrote a number of successful books about foreign policy. He was highly sought after by the press for his expertise in foreign affairs. People began to remember that he had done some good while in office. Still, he lived the rest of his life in the shadow of Watergate. He died in New York City on April 22, 1994. His funeral was attended by leaders from around the world, including every living U.S. president.

RICHARD M. NIXON

GLOSSARY

★ ★ ★

attorney general—a state or nation's top lawyer

candidate—someone running for office in an election

committees—groups of people working together on a project

communist—a system in which the government owns a country's businesses and controls the economy; a person who supports communist governments

conservative—believing that the government should have a limited role in people's lives

debate—a formal argument

foreign affairs—issues regarding countries' relations with each other

impeach—to charge a public official with a serious crime

nuclear weapons—powerful weapons that can destroy a large area

pardon—act that forgives a crime, so that the person who committed the crime is not punished

Soviet Union—a nation formed in 1922 when Russia combined with other countries in Eastern Europe and central Asia; it broke apart in 1991

RICHARD M. NIXON'S LIFE AT A GLANCE

★ ★ ★

PERSONAL

Nickname:	Tricky Dick
Born:	January 9, 1913
Birthplace:	Yorba Linda, California
Father's name:	Francis Anthony Nixon
Mother's name:	Hannah Milhous Nixon
Education:	Graduated from Whittier College in 1934 and from Duke University Law School in 1937
Wife's name:	Thelma Catherine "Pat" Ryan Nixon (1912–1993)
Married:	June 2, 1940
Children:	Patricia Nixon Cox (1946–); Julie Nixon Eisenhower (1948–)
Died:	April 22, 1994, in New York City
Buried:	Yorba Linda, California

PUBLIC

Occupation before presidency: Lawyer, public official

Occupation after presidency: Writer, foreign policy analyst

Military service: Lieutenant commander in the U.S. Navy during World War II

Other government positions: U.S. representative from California; U.S. senator from California; vice president

Political party: Republican

Vice presidents: Spiro T. Agnew (1969–1973); Gerald R. Ford (1973–1974)

Dates in office: January 20, 1969–August 9, 1974

Presidential opponents: John F. Kennedy (Democrat) (1960); Hubert H. Humphrey (Democrat) and George C. Wallace (American Independent), 1968; George McGovern (Democrat), 1972

Number of votes (Electoral College): 34,108,157 of 68,334,888 (219 of 522), 1960; 31,785,480 of 72,967,119 (301 of 538), 1968; 41,167,319 of 70,335,828 (520 of 538), 1972

Selected Writings: *Six Crises* (1962), *RN: The Memoirs of Richard Nixon* (1978), *In the Arena* (1990), *Beyond Peace* (1994)

★

Richard Milhous Nixon's Cabinet

Secretary of state:
William P. Rogers (1969–1973)
Henry A. Kissinger (1973–1974)
Secretary of the treasury:
David M. Kennedy (1969–1970)
John B. Connally Jr. (1971–1972)
George P. Schultz (1972–1974)
William E. Simon (1974)
Secretary of defense:
Melvin R. Laird (1969–1972)
Elliot L. Richardson (1973)
James R. Schlesinger (1973–1974)
Attorney general:
John N. Mitchell (1969–1972)
Richard G. Kleindienst (1972–1973)
Elliot L. Richardson (1973)
William B. Saxbe (1974)
Postmaster general:
Winton M. Blount (1969–1971)
Secretary of the interior:
Walter J. Hickel (1969–1970)
Rogers C. B. Morton (1971–1974)
Secretary of agriculture:
Clifford M. Hardin (1969–1971)
Earl L. Butz (1971–1974)
Secretary of commerce:
Maurice H. Stans (1969–1972)
Peter G. Peterson (1972)
Frederick B. Dent (1973–1974)
Secretary of labor:
George P. Schultz (1969–1970)
James D. Hodgson (1970–1972)
Peter J. Brennan (1973–1974)
Secretary of health, education, and welfare:
Robert H. Finch (1969–1970)
Elliot L. Richardson (1970–1973)
Caspar W. Weinberger (1973–1974)
Secretary of housing and urban development:
George W. Romney (1969–1972)
James T. Lynn (1973–1974)
Secretary of transportation:
John A. Volpe (1969–1973)
Claude S. Brinegar (1973–1974)

RICHARD M. NIXON'S LIFE AND TIMES

★ ★ ★

NIXON'S LIFE			WORLD EVENTS
January 9, Nixon is born in Yorba Linda, California	1913		
		1920	1920 American women get the right to vote
		1930	
Graduates from Whittier College	1934		
			1935 George Gershwin's *Porgy and Bess* opera opens in New York
Receives his law degree from Duke University (below)	1937		
			1939 Hollywood produces the film version of *Gone with the Wind*
			Commercial television is introduced to America
			The film *The Wizard of Oz* is released

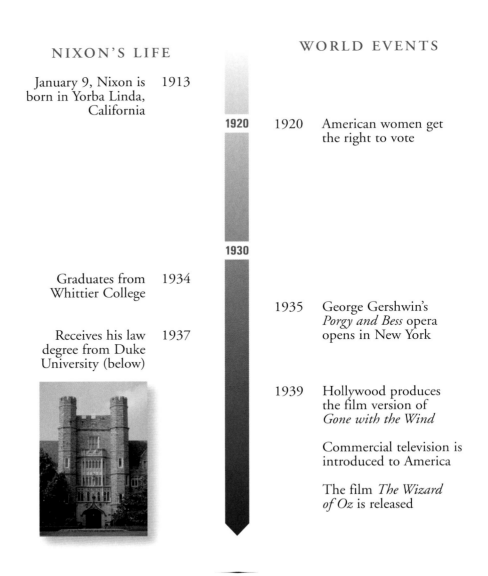

NIXON'S LIFE

June 21, marries 1940
Thelma Catherine
"Pat" Ryan (below)

Joins the navy 1942

Elected to the 1946
U.S. House of
Representatives
from California

WORLD EVENTS

1940

1941 December 7, Japanese
bombers attack Pearl
Harbor, Hawaii (below),
and America enters
World War II

1944 DNA (deoxyribonucleic
acid) is found to be
the basis of heredity

1945 The United Nations
is founded

1949 Birth of the People's
Republic of China

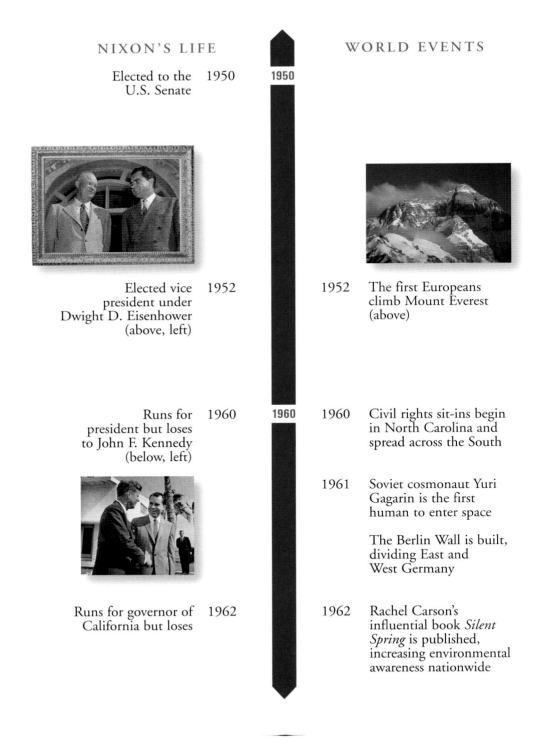

NIXON'S LIFE

Elected to the 1950
U.S. Senate

Elected vice 1952
president under
Dwight D. Eisenhower
(above, left)

Runs for 1960
president but loses
to John F. Kennedy
(below, left)

Runs for governor of 1962
California but loses

WORLD EVENTS

1950

1952   The first Europeans
       climb Mount Everest
       (above)

1960   Civil rights sit-ins begin
       in North Carolina and
       spread across the South

1961   Soviet cosmonaut Yuri
       Gagarin is the first
       human to enter space

       The Berlin Wall is built,
       dividing East and
       West Germany

1962   Rachel Carson's
       influential book *Silent
       Spring* is published,
       increasing environmental
       awareness nationwide

NIXON'S LIFE

Presidential Election Results:	Popular Votes	Electoral Votes
1968		
Richard M. Nixon	31,785,480	301
Hubert H. Humphrey	31,275,166	191
George C. Wallace	9,906,473	46

1969 Begins the slow withdrawal of U.S. troops from Vietnam

1970 The U.S. military begins attacking supply lines in Cambodia (above)

The National Guard kills four students during a Vietnam War protest at Kent State University

Creates the Environmental Protection Agency

1970

WORLD EVENTS

1968 Civil rights leader Martin Luther King Jr. (below) is shot and killed

1969 U.S. astronauts are the first humans to land on the moon (below)

1970 Earth Day is celebrated for the first time, promoting environmental awareness worldwide

The *Apollo 13* space mission is launched from Cape Kennedy, Florida

NIXON'S LIFE

Presidential Election Results:		Popular Votes	Electoral Votes
1972	Richard M. Nixon	41,167,319	520
	George McGovern	29,168,509	17
	John Hospers	—	1

February, visits China   1972

June 17, burglars break into the Democratic Party headquarters in the Watergate Hotel

January 27, a cease-fire is declared in the Vietnam War   1973

October, Congress begins impeachment hearings

October 10, Spiro Agnew resigns as vice president

December 6, Gerald Ford becomes vice president

August 9, resigns the presidency; Gerald Ford becomes president   1974

September 8, Ford pardons Nixon

WORLD EVENTS

1971   Gloria Steinem founds *Ms.* magazine, part of the women's liberation movement of the time

The first microprocessor is produced by Intel (below)

1973   Arab oil embargo creates concerns about natural resources

Spanish artist Pablo Picasso (below) dies

1974   Scientists find that chlorofluorocarbons—chemicals in coolants and propellants—are damaging to Earth's ozone layer

NIXON'S LIFE		WORLD EVENTS

Publishes several books, including *Leaders* (1982), *Real Peace: A Strategy for the West* (1983), and *No More Vietnams* (1985) — 1980-1989 — **1980**

1982 — Maya Lin designs the Vietnam War Memorial, commemorating the Americans who died

1983 — The AIDS (acquired immune deficiency syndrome) virus is identified

1986 — The U.S. Space Shuttle *Challenger* explodes, killing all seven astronauts on board (below)

Richard Nixon Library and Birthplace opens in Yorba Linda, California — 1990

1991 — Conflict between Iraq and Kuwait in the Persian Gulf begins

April 22, dies in New York City — 1994

1996 — Dolly (below), a sheep, is cloned in Scotland

UNDERSTANDING RICHARD M. NIXON AND HIS PRESIDENCY

★ ★ ★

IN THE LIBRARY

Dudley, Mark E. *United States v. Richard Nixon: Presidential Powers.* New York: Twenty-First Century Books, 1995.

Joseph, Paul. *Richard Nixon.* Minneapolis: Checkerboard Library, 1999.

Schuman, Michael A. *Richard M. Nixon.* Springfield, N.J.: Enslow, 1998.

ON THE WEB

For more information on *Richard M. Nixon*, use FactHound to track down Web sites related to this book.

1. Go to *www.facthound.com*
2. Type in this book ID: 0756502810
3. Click on the *Fetch It* button.

Your trusty FactHound will fetch the best Web sites for you!

NIXON HISTORIC SITES
ACROSS THE COUNTRY

Richard Nixon Library & Birthplace
18001 Yorba Linda Boulevard
Yorba Linda, CA 92886
714/903-3393
To see items from Nixon's childhood and presidency

THE U.S. PRESIDENTS
(Years in Office)

★ ★ ★

1. **George Washington**
   (March 4, 1789–March 3, 1797)
2. **John Adams**
   (March 4, 1797–March 3, 1801)
3. **Thomas Jefferson**
   (March 4, 1801–March 3, 1809)
4. **James Madison**
   (March 4, 1809–March 3, 1817)
5. **James Monroe**
   (March 4, 1817–March 3, 1825)
6. **John Quincy Adams**
   (March 4, 1825–March 3, 1829)
7. **Andrew Jackson**
   (March 4, 1829–March 3, 1837)
8. **Martin Van Buren**
   (March 4, 1837–March 3, 1841)
9. **William Henry Harrison**
   (March 6, 1841–April 4, 1841)
10. **John Tyler**
    (April 6, 1841–March 3, 1845)
11. **James K. Polk**
    (March 4, 1845–March 3, 1849)
12. **Zachary Taylor**
    (March 5, 1849–July 9, 1850)
13. **Millard Fillmore**
    (July 10, 1850–March 3, 1853)
14. **Franklin Pierce**
    (March 4, 1853–March 3, 1857)
15. **James Buchanan**
    (March 4, 1857–March 3, 1861)
16. **Abraham Lincoln**
    (March 4, 1861–April 15, 1865)
17. **Andrew Johnson**
    (April 15, 1865–March 3, 1869)

18. **Ulysses S. Grant**
    (March 4, 1869–March 3, 1877)
19. **Rutherford B. Hayes**
    (March 4, 1877–March 3, 1881)
20. **James Garfield**
    (March 4, 1881–Sept 19, 1881)
21. **Chester Arthur**
    (Sept 20, 1881–March 3, 1885)
22. **Grover Cleveland**
    (March 4, 1885–March 3, 1889)
23. **Benjamin Harrison**
    (March 4, 1889–March 3, 1893)
24. **Grover Cleveland**
    (March 4, 1893–March 3, 1897)
25. **William McKinley**
    (March 4, 1897–
    September 14, 1901)
26. **Theodore Roosevelt**
    (September 14, 1901–
    March 3, 1909)
27. **William Howard Taft**
    (March 4, 1909–March 3, 1913)
28. **Woodrow Wilson**
    (March 4, 1913–March 3, 1921)
29. **Warren G. Harding**
    (March 4, 1921–August 2, 1923)
30. **Calvin Coolidge**
    (August 3, 1923–March 3, 1929)
31. **Herbert Hoover**
    (March 4, 1929–March 3, 1933)
32. **Franklin D. Roosevelt**
    (March 4, 1933–April 12, 1945)

33. **Harry S. Truman**
    (April 12, 1945–
    January 20, 1953)
34. **Dwight D. Eisenhower**
    (January 20, 1953–
    January 20, 1961)
35. **John F. Kennedy**
    (January 20, 1961–
    November 22, 1963)
36. **Lyndon B. Johnson**
    (November 22, 1963–
    January 20, 1969)
37. **Richard M. Nixon**
    (January 20, 1969–
    August 9, 1974)
38. **Gerald R. Ford**
    (August 9, 1974–
    January 20, 1977)
39. **James Earl Carter**
    (January 20, 1977–
    January 20, 1981)
40. **Ronald Reagan**
    (January 20, 1981–
    January 20, 1989)
41. **George H. W. Bush**
    (January 20, 1989–
    January 20, 1993)
42. **William Jefferson Clinton**
    (January 20, 1993–
    January 20, 2001)
43. **George W. Bush**
    (January 20, 2001–)

INDEX

★ ★ ★

ABOUT THE AUTHOR

Robert Green holds a master's degree in journalism from New York University and a bachelor's degree in English literature from Boston University. He has also studied Chinese in Taiwan.

Green is the author of *Theodore Roosevelt* and *Woodrow Wilson* in this series. He has also written twenty other nonfiction books for young readers, including *Modern Nations of the World: China* and *Modern Nations of the World: Taiwan,* as well as biographies of historical figures including Julius Caesar, Cleopatra, Alexander the Great, Tutankhamun, Herod the Great, and Hannibal.